10 MYSTERIES OF THE CHRISTIAN FAITH

By

Rev. Anthony Mucciolo DD

Mucciolo Publishing
Glenolden, Pa. 19036

Mucciolo Publishing
Glenolden, Pa. 19036

DEDICATION

I want to dedicate this book to my entire family, far and near, all my children and grandchildren, and to all the friends God has so graciously given me in this life— both here in America—and in Bethlehem, a city located in the West Bank of the Palestinian territory.

It is my sincere prayer that God's Vision and Plan which he has pre-determined in Christ Jesus will be executed in these days for his Holy Name's sake, and for the benefit of all the children of God.

FOREWORD

Ultimately, a mystery is the concealment of some fact or truth. Theologians and clerics with the knowledge of the Christian faith from its inception have apparently decided that it is in the best interest of the Church to keep certain truths hidden. It is my belief that God would not have revealed what he chose to keep hidden. The Mystery of the Gospel is one such example. God kept this mystery hidden from every being he created from the foundation of the earth; but revealed it to the Church shortly after the resurrection. This revelation was intended not only to defeat the enemies of our souls, but also to humiliate them. Therefore, to keep this mystery a secret brings great dishonor and discredit to the Lord of Glory.

I believe that a vast number of Christians will be well served to have these mysteries revealed to them. The purpose is to draw each one into an intimate relationship with the Lord, for there is nothing greater on earth.

MYSTERY OF SALVATION

You've probably heard this message a hundred times or more, that Jesus died for our sins and rose from the dead; but have you heard the rest of the story? Do you know what Jesus was doing from the time he took his last earthly breath until his resurrection? He was fulfilling the great mystery of salvation that God kept secret from before the foundation of the earth.

On the first day, we know that Jesus entered Paradise accompanied by the thief on the cross. On this day, Jesus would reveal himself to the deceased prophets and believers in the God of Abraham.

> And Jesus said unto him, Verily I say unto thee, To day shalt thou be with me in paradise. (Luke 23:43)

Then, on the second day, he began to dismantle the kingdom of darkness beginning with those souls who were held captive by the powers of darkness in the depths of the earth when He went to visit the spirits held in prison.

> By which also he went and preached unto the spirits in prison; Which sometime were

disobedient, when once the longsuffering of God waited in the days of Noah, while the ark was a preparing, wherein few, that is, eight souls were saved by water. (1 Pet 3:19,20)

For this cause was the gospel preached also to them that are dead, that they might be judged according to men in the flesh, but live according to God in the spirit. (1 Pet 4:6)

He did something more on the second day; for he also fulfilled the mystery of the Gospel. The answer to the question—What is this mystery — also provides the best evidence that Christianity is indeed the only true faith. What makes it so? It is the revelation of a magnificent work by the God of Abraham, Isaac, and Jacob that is not attributed to any other god and is not taught by any other religion. Surely, you will gain a clearer understanding of the New Testament writings of Paul as I refer back to his many teachings on several subjects.

Howbeit we speak wisdom among them that are perfect [perfected]: yet not the wisdom of this world, nor of the princes of this world, that come to naught: But we speak the wisdom of God in a mystery, even the hidden wisdom, which God ordained before the world unto our glory: Which none of the princes of this world knew: for had they known it, they would not have crucified the Lord of glory. (1 Cor 2:2-8)

According to the Scriptures, Lucifer was perfect in wisdom (Ezek.28:3); there was no secret thing withheld from him except this one grand mystery. Truly, he never would have crucified the Lord if he knew the disaster it would bring to his kingdom.

"For this reason I, Paul, the prisoner of Christ Jesus for the sake of you Gentiles—Surely you have heard about the administration of God's grace that was given to me for you, that is, the mystery made known to me by revelation, as I have already written briefly. In reading this, then, you will be able to understand my insight into the mystery of Christ, which was not made known to men in other generations as it has now been revealed by the Spirit to God's holy apostles and prophets. **This mystery is that through the gospel the Gentiles are heirs together with Israel, members together of one body, and sharers together in the promise in Christ Jesus.** *I became a servant of this*

*gospel by the gift of God's grace given me through the working of his power. Although I am less than the least of all God's people, this grace was given me: to preach to the Gentiles the unsearchable riches of Christ, and to make plain to everyone the administration of this mystery, which for ages past was kept hidden in God, who created all things. **His intent was that now, through the church, the manifold wisdom of God should be made known to the rulers and authorities in the heavenly realms, according to his eternal purpose which he accomplished in Christ Jesus our Lord.** In him and through faith in him we may approach God with freedom and confidence."* (Eph 3:1-12 NIV)

The revelation and administration of this mystery was the true and unifying message of salvation to Jew and Gentile alike. Believing that Jesus Christ existed in the flesh and the historical accounts of his works alone apparently was not enough to embolden a believer to walk into an arena knowing he is about to be devoured by lions. There had to be something more engaging, more significant.

This great mystery is intended to be declared in every church to the embarrassment and humiliation of the forces of darkness. *God's intent was that now, through the church, the manifold wisdom of God should be made known to the rulers and authorities in the heavenly realms.* Personally, I can't recall ever hearing a message that would embarrass the devil. If we speak evil of him, he is glorified in the evil; and if we speak well of him, he is glorified as well. So what could we say or do that would humiliate him?

Unknown to the principalities, dominions and thrones in high places at the time of Christ, unless this mystery was fulfilled, no one, especially the Gentiles, could be saved. Although this act of great love is virtually unknown to the Church today, it was truly the power of the Living God preparing the way for the salvation of both the Jew and Gentile, whereby we are made one by his sacrifice at Calvary.

So, what is the Mystery of the Gospel? Remember these verses? *"Now is the judgment of this world: now shall the prince of this world be cast out. And I, if I be lifted up from the earth, will draw all men unto me."* (John 12:31,32) Jesus spoke these words a few days before his crucifixion. "Now shall the prince of this world be cast out." Was Satan cast out from the earth? That's what he said; but how, when? Many have argued in their ignorance that since Jesus Christ was crucified, all men have not been drawn to him. The fact is, all mankind was drawn to him at the execution of the mystery. On the second day, Jesus ascended to the stratosphere and engulfed the entire earth in his light

Consequently, there was no place found for the princes of darkness to hide. Every wicked throne was cast down to the ground and every prince and demon of darkness was cast out of the earth. Lastly, Satan himself was cast out. He lost his control over all souls, those who died before and those who would die thereafter in Christ. Every human being and their future seed were covered in his light; for all sin, offenses, and transgression were forgiven and washed away by the blood of the Lamb. It was at this moment that all flesh was drawn to him by the washing of sanctification and regeneration. From that time to the present day, Lucifer must go about like a roaring lion seeking whom he may devour because every believer is invisible to him by virtue of the Light and living blood of our Savior. This is why it is important that we remain in Christ and covered by the blood, the eternal light of our Lord Jesus Christ.

> *"And without controversy great is the mystery of godliness: God was manifest in the flesh, justified in the Spirit, seen of angels, preached unto the Gentiles, believed on in the world, received up into glory."*
> (1 Tim 3:16)

God was received up into glory? It was the Spirit of God that dwelt in Christ that ascended to the heavens above the earth and eliminated the powers of darkness. Here is where all the doctrines concerning Jesus Christ come together. If we are confused, it isn't because the Lord would have us perplexed; but, that for generations the debates over the identity of Jesus Christ have raged on. The Scriptures inform us that Jesus is part of the Godhead, the Son of God who was conceived – not by the seed of man, but by the Spirit of God; that he was slain before the earth was created, but manifested in these days for our salvation, and resurrected with a new body, while retaining the scars of the old. Hence, we need to look at him with a much clearer vision. In the letters of Paul, Jesus and the Father are often pictured as one and the same; adding to the claim of Jesus who said, *"I and the Father are one"* and, *"When you see me, you see the Father."*

Consider this: The vast majority of saints who became martyrs for the cause of Christ never witnessed the resurrection. They heard about it through the apostles, and were convinced that God had showed them great mercy in saving their souls from death. They were taught the meaning of these words: *"In Him was Life; and the Life was the Light of men"*. (Jn.1:4)

To the glory of the Father in Christ, his sacrifice at Calvary made salvation available to all; not just the Jew, not just a few, but every soul that would ever exist or had existed on earth as well; for whosoever receives him, to them he gives the power to become the children of God, the children and sons of the Light. Now, what other religion can give their god the glory for performing this great work of salvation; and how will they document this great act of love if they tried to incorporate it in their teachings? To this day, only Christianity has ever documented God's work of salvation in Christ Jesus. Truly, I can say with all certainty and with great emphasis that Jesus Christ is the Lord; even the same who sits at the right hand of God's majesty on high.

Now I can understand why the martyrs walked into the arenas with their heads held high. They knew that they were clothed in the Light, adorned with the garments of salvation, and freed from the jaws of the lion that wanted to devour their souls. They were confident that as He lives, so they would live, and as He was resurrected, so they would be resurrected. They weren't going to their death; they were walking into Life, and into the arms of him whose death and resurrection made it possible for them to enter glory.

With this understanding of the mystery of the Gospel, the saints of old considered it a great honor to walk as children of Light and rejected the inclinations to walk in darkness. This was their confidence. They were children of the Light, and while it may appear that darkness had fallen upon them, they were able to sing the song of David as they entered the arena, and quote the anthem of their immortality, Psalm 91.

They had the vision of life: and while the Jews are destined to remain blind to this gospel until the last Gentile enters the kingdom, the Light of Life indwells a large number of their souls and gives them the spiritual strength to remain steadfast in their belief in the God of Abraham, the Father of Christ Jesus. I wish I could say that the Light of Life indwelled them all, but unfortunately I can't.

Now if God gave his Son so that whosoever believes in him should not perish, and gave us the right to walk in his Light for the eternal salvation of our souls, then should we not be filled with gratitude for his precious gift and refuse to walk in sin to the glory of Satan? To be saved from worldly infirmities, we must walk in his Light, his covering of salvation, with the garments of sanctification adorned as a bride walking towards the altar of marriage, surrendering our lives to him, and remaining with him forever, having been justified by his blood.

The next question is a personal one – ask yourselves — Am I willing to acknowledge the Lord Jesus Christ and God the Father as my Lord and Savior and walk in gratitude for the mighty work of salvation that he fulfilled for me so that I may enjoy a relationship with Him and enter eternal life? You may say, "I would have to give up so much (sinning) to surrender my life to the Lord." Jesus gave his life and shed his blood so you can live. Are you willing to walk away from so great a gift for the pleasures of this life?

"But I do my best to live a decent life. I don't steal, lie, or cheat. I don't go out of my way to hurt people or kill anyone. What does God want from me to prove my love for him?" The first act of faith is to ask God to forgive your rebelliousness and rejection of Him, and His word, which is the sin unto death, and to forgive all your offenses and transgressions. Acknowledge his sacrifice on the cross whereby He gave His life so that you may live, and ask him to come and dwell in your heart. This is only the beginning. Allow God to dwell in your heart and cover you with His Light. For greater is he that is in you, than he that is in the world. By his Light, you will be protected from the forces of evil that desire your soul. Next, you will learn why you need to be grateful and respectful, which is the second greatest act of love for the Lord.

VENERATION

All the truths regarding veneration are not openly disclosed, therefore its truths remain a mystery. Veneration is a condition of the heart; a state of mind, the inspiration and motivation of the Spirit. It is one of the main fruits of salvation. Veneration of the Lord requires us to make conscious decisions, namely; having an intense desire for a deep, personal union with the Lord; and a yearning to trust his word. These decisions must be manifested in the new believer before "veneration" or "true worship" is possible. These are the ones God seeks after – those who will worship him in Spirit and in Truth – those who will venerate him.

The ability to worship the Lord as he truly desires to be worshipped requires a maturing spiritual growth. What is the first phase of our growth in Christ? The answer is learning to RESPECT him. It is written that *the fear of the LORD is the beginning of knowledge: but fools despise wisdom and instruction.* (Prov 1:7) The word "fear" in the Hebrew tongue also means respect and reverence. Reverence is a synonym for veneration. We must question our attitude towards the Scriptures. Has it changed since accepting Christ? It should have because the seal of the Holy Spirit prompts us to feed on the Word. Without a respect and reverence for the Lord, we can never enter the realm of understanding, knowledge and/or truth. Consider the truth of this statement— if we don't have respect for someone, it is virtually impossible to love them with all of our heart, soul, mind, and strength, a love which the Lord desires first and foremost.

So, how do we learn to respect the Lord if we don't have a true knowledge of Him? That is a good question. In order for us to know him we need to eat and drink His word daily. As you read, set your mind on obeying the commandments and teachings of the Lord: not as a legal mandate, but out of a desire to show respect for his word. True growth in Christ is found in one fulfilling the law of Christ out of a freewill spirit, not bound by ecclesiastical mandates. What kind of love would we have for our spouse if we were just trying to fulfill a law that says we must? Would it result in a true love for the other? It is written as a commandment that we should love the Lord our God with all of our heart, soul, mind, and strength. However, this is not a "commandment" to fulfill an act of love in the traditional sense; rather, it is the goal set forth for all God's people. Without a true respect for the Lord, veneration and adoration is impossible. Its reality remains very much a mystery to us.

Too often we hear it said, "Find a Bible believing church," but what we should say is "Find a church whose pastor is spiritually driven to teach the people **how to** develop a close and personal relationship with the Lord." It's not enough to say, "You gotta read the Bible: You gotta walk in righteousness," etc. The true pastor who has been called by God will teach us **"how to do"** all the things God requires of us because he, himself, has matured in the faith and knowledge of Christ.

In the early church, the new convert spent two to three hours every night of the week praying with and listening to the teachings of the disciples. Here is an example of a teaching to the new catechists (converts) encouraging them to listen to wholesome words:

> "As the Scripture says, "Anyone who trusts in him will never be put to shame." For there is no difference between Jew and Gentile-- the same Lord is Lord of all and richly blesses all who call on him, for, "Everyone who calls on the name of the Lord will be saved." How, then, can they call on the one they have not believed in? And how can they believe in the one of whom they have not heard? And how can they hear without someone preaching to them? And how can they preach unless they are sent? As it is written, "How beautiful are the feet of those who bring good news!" (Rom. 10:11-15 NIV)

> *It was he who gave some to be apostles, some to be prophets, some to be evangelists, and some to be pastors and teachers, <u>**to prepare God's people for works of service, so that the body of Christ may be built up until we all reach unity in the faith and in the knowledge of the Son of God and become mature,**</u> attaining to the whole measure of the fullness of Christ.* (Eph.4:11-13 NIV)

The whole purpose of the ministry is not telling us what we "gotta do" or what we "gotta have", but rather, to lead us in developing our faith, our reverence, our righteousness, etc. until we become mature in our love for the Lord.

> *Then we will no longer be infants, tossed back and forth by the waves, and blown here and there by every wind of teaching and by the cunning and craftiness of men in their deceitful scheming. Instead, speaking the truth in love, we will in all things grow up into him who is the Head, that is, Christ. From him the whole body, joined and held together by every supporting ligament, grows and builds itself up in love, as each part does its work.* (Eph. 4:14 -16 NIV)

Respect and gratitude refer to a state of mind. "Why do you call me, 'Lord, Lord,' and do not do what I say?" ("Luke 6:46 NIV) the Lord asks. If we are to develop this mindset, we must be willing to turn away from the way we used to live and walk according to the teachings of the new way of life in Christ. He has removed our old filthy rags of unrighteousness and adorned us with the pure white garments of salvation. Would it be a show of respect and gratitude to remove his garments and go back to the old filthy rags we wore in the past? In the days of the apostle's teachings, the new convert merely needed to observe the intensity and adoration that the Lord's disciple displayed in his worship to discern his own spiritual growth.

In Paul's teachings to the Ephesians chapters 4 and 5, there is a laundry list of do's and don'ts imparted to the new convert. St. Paul and his flock of pastors did not have huge, ornate churches with enormous mortgages, salaries, and other bills that caused them to be concerned if they lost some tithers. They were strictly sold out to God who demanded an accounting of the sheep and their spiritual growth. I'm going to number each of these do's and don'ts which will not correlate with the actual Scripture verses; rather they will serve as a list of things the pastors and converts were focused on both in prayer and in teaching. These were the stepping stones to true worship and veneration in the Spirit.

*So I tell you this, and insist on it in the Lord,
(1)* **that you must no longer live as the
Gentiles do**, *in the futility of their thinking.
They are darkened in their understanding
and* **separated from the life of God because
of the ignorance that is in them due to the
stubbornness of their hearts.** *Having lost all
sensitivity, they have given themselves over
to sensuality so as to indulge in every kind of
impurity, with a continual lust for more. You,
however, did not come to know Christ that
way. Surely you heard of him and were
taught in him in accordance with the truth
that is in Jesus. (2)* **You were taught,** *with
regard to your former way of life,* **to put off
your old self, which is being corrupted by its
deceitful desires; (3) to be made new in the
attitude of your minds; and (4) to put on the
new self, created to be like God in true
righteousness and holiness.** *(5) Therefore
each of you must put off falsehood and (6)
speak truthfully to his neighbor, for we are
all members of one body. (7)"In your anger
do not sin": (8) do not let the sun go down
while you are still angry, and (9) do not give
the devil a foothold. (10) He who has been
stealing must steal no longer, but must work,
doing something useful with his own hands,
that he may have something to share with*

those in need. (11) Do not let any unwholesome talk come out of your mouths, but (12) only what is helpful for building others up according to their needs, that it may benefit those who listen. (13) And do not grieve the Holy Spirit of God, with whom you were sealed for the day of redemption. (14) **Get rid of all bitterness, (15) rage and anger, (16) brawling and slander, (17) along with every form of malice. (18) Be kind and compassionate to one another, (19) forgiving each other, just as in Christ God forgave you. (20) Be imitators of God, therefore, as dearly loved children and (21) live a life of love, just as Christ loved us and gave himself up for us as a fragrant offering and sacrifice to God. (22) But among you there must not be even a hint of sexual immorality, (23) or of any kind of impurity, or of greed, because these are improper for God's holy people.** *(24) Nor should there be obscenity, (25) foolish talk or coarse joking, which are out of place, but rather (26) thanksgiving.* **For of this you can be sure: no immoral, impure or greedy person — such a man is an idolater — has any inheritance in the kingdom of Christ and of God.** *(27) Let no one deceive you with empty words, for because of such things God's wrath comes* *on those who are disobedient. (28) Therefore do not be partners with them.* **For you were once darkness, but now you are light in the Lord. (29) Live as children of light (for the fruit of the light consists in all goodness, righteousness and truth and (30) find out what pleases the Lord.** *(31) Have nothing to do with the fruitless deeds of darkness, but (32) rather expose them. (33) For it is shameful even to mention what the disobedient do in secret. But everything exposed by the light becomes visible, for it is light that makes everything visible. This is why it is said: "Wake up, O sleeper, rise from the dead, and Christ will shine on you. (34) Be very careful, then, how you live — (35) not as unwise but as wise, making the most of every opportunity, because the days are evil. (36) Therefore do not be foolish, but (37) understand what the Lord's will is. (38) Do not get drunk on wine, which leads to debauchery. Instead, (39) be filled with the Spirit.* (Eph.4:17-5:18 NIV)*

It was very common for a believer to confess to the pastor and elders that he was having a problem with his anger, for example. The ministry devoted many hours in prayer as was needed to break the power of the man's rage. Sometimes it took months of daily prayer and many days of fasting as well before the power of rage and bitterness could be broken, but they never gave up. The same held true for those who wanted to be filled with the Holy Spirit and the vitality that is in Christ Jesus.

God wants our hearts to be filled with adoration and admiration of him. A heart filled with love and the words of the Most High makes it a joy to worship, adore, magnify and glorify the Lord of glory. Jesus Christ becomes the receiver of our worship and veneration; and we become the receiver of his blessings and gifts. Veneration of the Lord also requires us to learn and fulfill the mystery of holiness and Godliness which I will discuss in the next chapter.

GODLINESS

And without controversy great is the mystery of godliness: God was manifest in the flesh, justified in the Spirit, seen of angels, preached unto the Gentiles, believed on in the world, received up into glory. (1 Tim 3:16) The mystery of Godliness paved the way for the next set of disciplines each convert was required to learn, put into practice, and develop a passion for. Among these was a life committed to holiness. In first century Christendom, holiness was considered a sacred trust that God vested in the new believers endowing them with obligations to honor its sanctity. It was not an option one may choose to obey or refuse to observe. Holiness was the glove, or outward expression, and Godliness was the hand, or Spirit.

In the modern Christian church, it is commonly taught that holiness is abstention from evil and includes the performance of deeds worthy of God's notice. In their simplicity these statements are valid, but they are lacking the essence of the earliest truths. Holiness is the sacred essence of Almighty God that is imputed to the new convert, shielding his soul from evil and permitting him to approach the Living God, be recognized, and have his prayers received with respect. Holiness results in one abstaining from evil; but abstaining from evil does not make one holy. Holiness and Godliness are the newly adorned garments of sanctification we are dressed with after we are washed in the blood of the Lamb.

I have put together an exposé of what the new convert to the gospel of Jesus Christ would have experienced as he attended one of the church gatherings mentored by the Disciples of Christ. In this scenario, Paul and Peter will present their instructions on holiness to the church body. Paul speaks first and is not shy about reminding them of the [mystery of the Gospel] fulfilled by God in Christ. These teachings are found in their letters to the churches.

At one time we too were foolish, disobedient, deceived and enslaved by all kinds of passions and pleasures. We lived in malice and envy, being hated and hating one another. But when the kindness and love of God our Savior appeared, he saved us, not because of righteous things we had done, but because of his mercy. He saved us through the washing of rebirth and renewal by the Holy Spirit, whom he poured out on us generously through Jesus Christ our Savior, so that, having been justified by his grace, we might become heirs having the hope of eternal life. (Titus 3:3-7 NIV)

And we pray this in order that you may live a life worthy of the Lord and may please him in every way: bearing fruit in every good work, growing in the knowledge of God, being strengthened with all power according to his glorious might so that you may have great endurance and patience, and joyfully giving thanks to the Father, who has qualified you to share in the inheritance of the saints in the kingdom of light. (Col.1:10-12 NIV)

According to Paul, Godliness is the pathway to the Father allowing us to grow in the knowledge of him, and to be strengthened in the inner man with great patience and endurance. This was part of the message of faith to ground the new believer as he struggled to be free of the desires of his earthly nature.

For he has rescued us from the dominion of darkness and brought us into the kingdom of the Son he loves, in whom we have redemption, the forgiveness of sins. He is the image of the invisible God, the firstborn over all creation. For by him all things were created: things in heaven and on earth, visible and invisible, whether thrones or powers or rulers or authorities; all things were created by him and for him. He is before all things, and in him all things hold together. And he is the head of the body, the church; he is the beginning and the firstborn from among the dead, so that in everything he might have the supremacy. For God was pleased to have all his fullness dwell in him, and through him to reconcile to himself all things, whether things on earth or things in heaven, by making peace through his blood, shed on the cross. Once you were alienated from God and were enemies in your minds because of your evil behavior. But now he has reconciled you by Christ's physical body through death to present you holy in his sight, without blemish and free from accusation--if you continue in your faith, established and firm, not moved from the hope held out in the gospel. (Col.1:13-23)

As we see here, holiness is the covering that allows us to be brought into the presence of God without accusation, and having the endurance to remain firm in our determination to grow in the faith.

> *This is the gospel that you heard and that has been proclaimed to every creature under heaven, and of which I, Paul, have become a servant.* (Col 1:23 NIV)

> *And he made known to us the mystery of his will according to his good pleasure, which he purposed in Christ, to be put into effect when the times will have reached their fulfillment-- to bring all things in heaven and on earth together under one head, even Christ. In him we were also chosen, having been predestined according to the plan of him who works out everything in conformity with the purpose of his will, in order that we, who were the first to hope in Christ, might be for the praise of his glory. And you also were included in Christ when you heard the word of truth, the gospel of your salvation. Having believed, you were marked in him with a seal, the promised Holy Spirit, who is a deposit guaranteeing our inheritance until the redemption of those who are God's possession--to the praise of his glory.* (Eph 1:9-14 NIV)

So do not be ashamed to testify about our Lord, or ashamed of me his prisoner. But join with me in suffering for the gospel, by the power of God, who has saved us and called us to a holy life--not because of anything we have done but because of his own purpose and grace. This grace was given us in Christ Jesus before the beginning of time, but it has now been revealed through the appearing of our Savior, Christ Jesus, who has destroyed death and has brought life and immortality to light through the gospel. (2 Tim 1:8-10 NIV)

In this setting Paul walks to the side, sits down, and awaits the words of Peter, who now stands before the catechists.

Therefore, prepare your minds for action; be self-controlled; set your hope fully on the grace to be given you when Jesus Christ is revealed. As obedient children, do not conform to the evil desires you had when you lived in ignorance. But just as he who called you is holy, so be holy in all you do; for it is written: "Be holy, because I am holy." Since you call on a Father who judges each man's work impartially, live your lives as strangers here in reverent fear. For you know that it was not with perishable things such as silver or gold that you were redeemed from the empty way of life handed down to you from your forefathers, but with the precious blood of Christ, a lamb without blemish or defect. He was chosen before the creation of the world, but was revealed in these last times for your sake. Through him you believe in God, who raised him from the dead and glorified him, and so your faith and hope are in God. Now that you have purified yourselves by obeying the truth so that you have sincere love for your brothers, love one another deeply, from the heart. For you have been born again, not of perishable seed, but of imperishable, through the living and enduring word of God. For, "All men are like grass, and all their glory is like the flowers of the field; the grass withers and the flowers fall, but the word of the Lord stands forever." And this is the word that was preached to you. Therefore, rid yourselves of all malice and all deceit, hypocrisy, envy, and slander of every kind. Like newborn babies, crave pure spiritual milk, so that by it you may grow up in your salvation, now that you have tasted that the Lord is good. But you are a chosen people, a royal priesthood, a holy nation, a people belonging to God, that you may declare the praises of him who called you out of darkness into his wonderful light. Once you were not a people, but now you are the people of God; once you had not received mercy, but now you have received mercy. Dear friends, I urge you, as aliens and strangers in the world, to abstain from sinful desires, which war against your soul. (1 Pet 1:13 – 2:11 NIV)

As you have seen, it was absolutely imperative the new convert learn what was involved in holiness, and how it differed from what was common. He was educated in the sacredness of everything that God considered holy and he had to regard them with dignity and honor.

There were many things that were esteemed to be most holy, among which was a convert's vow of separation to seek the Lord with all his heart. This was a most holy practice and highly recommended to every believer who sought God's truth. The Covenants God made with Moses and Abraham were also most holy. The church body, the Temple of the Lord, was considered holy as well. In addition, they were given many more lessons to support the doctrine of holiness.

If any man defile the temple of God, him shall God destroy; for the temple of God is holy, which temple ye are. (1 Cor 3:17)

Food for the stomach and the stomach for food"—but God will destroy them both. The body is not meant for sexual immorality, but for the Lord, and the Lord for the body. By his power God raised the Lord from the dead, and he will raise us also. Do you not know that your bodies are members of Christ himself? Shall I then take the members of Christ and unite them with a prostitute? Never! Do you not know that he who unites himself with a prostitute is one with her in body? For it is said, "The two will become one flesh." But he who unites himself with the Lord is one with him in spirit. Flee from sexual immorality. All other sins a man commits are outside his body, but he who sins sexually sins against his own body. Do you not know that your body is a temple of the Holy Spirit, who is in you, whom you have received from God? You are not your own; you were bought at a price. Therefore honor God with your body.
(1 Cor 6:13-20 NIV)

One of the toughest challenges that confronts a man or a woman today is withdrawing from sexual relations with their partner; especially if they have strong feelings for each other. But, having premarital sex was not an option for the new converts. They could attend the teachings in hopes they would eventually convert, but they could not partake of the Communion of the saints. Marriage was the only acceptable option.

They were also taught not to be judgmental and high minded against the Jews; for they are part of the Israel of God and are holy and sacred to the Father. Paul strongly admonished them not to degrade the Jews; as pride and haughtiness defiled that which was made holy in Christ.

> *If the part of the dough offered as firstfruits is holy, then the whole batch is holy; if the root is holy, so are the branches. If some of the branches have been broken off, and you, though a wild olive shoot, have been grafted in among the others and now share in the nourishing sap from the olive root, do not boast over those branches. If you do, consider this: You do not support the root, but the root supports you. You will say then, "Branches were broken off so that I could be grafted in." Granted. But they were broken off because of unbelief, and you stand by faith. Do not be*

arrogant, but be afraid. For if God did not spare the natural branches, he will not spare you either. Consider therefore the kindness and sternness of God: sternness to those who fell, but kindness to you, provided that you continue in his kindness. Otherwise, you also will be cut off. And if they do not persist in unbelief, they will be grafted in, for God is able to graft them in again. After all, if you were cut out of an olive tree that is wild by nature, and contrary to nature were grafted into a cultivated olive tree, how much more readily will these, the natural branches, be grafted into their own olive tree! I do not want you to be ignorant of this mystery, brothers, so that you may not be conceited: Israel has experienced a hardening in part until the full number of the Gentiles has come in. And so all Israel will be saved, as it is written: "The deliverer will come from Zion; he will turn godlessness away from Jacob. And this is my covenant with them when I take away their sins." As far as the gospel is concerned, they are enemies on your account; but as far as election is concerned, they are loved on account of the patriarchs, for God's gifts and his call are irrevocable. Just as you who were at one time disobedient to God have now received mercy as a result of their disobedience, so they too have now become disobedient in order that they too may now receive mercy as a result of God's mercy to you. For God has bound all men over to disobedience so that he may have mercy on them all. (Rom 11:16-32 NIV)

The catechists entered the conclave just as new converts enter the church today with ideas and perceptions of how they were expected to live their lives; but they soon found out their views were grossly inadequate in comparison to the demands of true holiness and Godliness. Paul sent a message to the church in Colossae that mirrored his message to the Ephesians. However, he concentrated more on the need for charity and holiness.

Put to death, therefore, whatever belongs to your earthly nature: sexual immorality, impurity, lust, evil desires and greed, which is idolatry. Because of these, the wrath of God is coming. You used to walk in these ways, in the life you once lived. But now you must rid yourselves of all such things as these: anger, rage, malice, slander, and filthy language from your lips. Do not lie to each other, since you have taken off your old self with its

practices and have put on the new self, which is being renewed in knowledge in the image of its Creator. Here there is no Greek or Jew, circumcised or uncircumcised, barbarian, Scythian, slave or free, but Christ is all, and is in all. Therefore, as God's chosen people, holy and dearly loved, clothe yourselves with compassion, kindness, humility, gentleness and patience. Bear with each other and forgive whatever grievances you may have against one another. Forgive as the Lord forgave you. And over all these virtues put on love, which binds them all together in perfect unity. Let the peace of Christ rule in your hearts, since as members of one body you were called to peace. And be thankful. Let the word of Christ dwell in you richly as you teach and admonish one another with all wisdom, and as you sing psalms, hymns and spiritual songs with gratitude in your hearts to God. And whatever you do, whether in word or deed, do it all in the name of the Lord Jesus, giving thanks to God the Father through him.
(Col 3:5-17 NIV)

These were the Basic Instructions and Disciplines in Godliness taught to the children of God under the watchful eyes of the apostles and elders ordained for such purpose. With these instructions, the believer was taught what was necessary to develop a deep respect and reverence for the Father who had saved them with a mighty salvation in Christ.

Holiness draws the believer into a union with Christ, without whom holiness is non-existent. Christianity wasn't about warming the pews; it was a life worth living to the honor and glory of Almighty God in Christ who was renowned and worshipped for the great work of deliverance and salvation of their souls. They learned what it meant to "appreciate the blood" that was poured out for their sin.

If Christians were learning and abiding by these principles today, our country and the world would be a better place to live. There are other religions that demand holiness from its membership; but in Christ, the Father simply requires that whatever we do—let it be the result of the Holy Spirit working in us and giving us a "will to do" rather than a "command to do". Loving the Lord with all our hearts requires a heart desirous of showing love, not one strictly acting out of a commandment to love.

This lesson is not easy to master. This is why we need pastors who know how to teach these principles and drive the message into our hearts. Now we know that God not only wants respect, but He wants us to show our respect for Him by living in a state of holiness in honor of Him. This Godliness requires the wearing of the garments of holiness given to us by the Lord, himself, with honor and humility. This humility is given to us in through the work of charity which I will speak of in the next chapter. We must be willing to give the Lord what He desires in exchange for the life that He has planned for us.

Know and understand this. If you cannot find a pastor who is intent on conducting himself as the pastors in St. Paul's day, then you must take it upon yourself to pray and seek the Lord to overcome the deficiencies outlined in Ephesians and to seek the fullness of God's Holy Spirit. It is your responsibility to seek the Lord and work out your own salvation with reverence and respect for the one who has called you for such a time as this.

CHARITY

Charity is a mystery? Since the fullness of charity is not well known, its properties remain a mystery. We all believe that we know what charity is but perhaps by the time you finish this chapter you will have come to realize that the disciplines of the early church were progressive, built as lively stones one upon another. That is, you couldn't master one discipline without having the essence of another incorporated in its teaching. Godliness, for example, cannot be perfected without charity, and as we shall see, in order for charity to reach its high water mark, it must be accompanied by faith; one precious stone upon another creating a new temple unto the Lord; one precious pearl [doctrine] linked to the next creating a magnificent necklace of grace; and grace without charity is empty and void of life.

Where the Light of God makes us holy, charity provides a means for God's Light to shine through us to the world. It is the Light of God's glory that provides the evidence that the Spirit of Christ is in us. Charity is the Lord's garment of praise which includes all of the following according to the teachings of St. Paul.

> *Therefore, as God's chosen people,* **holy and dearly loved, (1) clothe yourselves with compassion, (2) kindness, (3) humility, (4) gentleness and (5) patience.** *(6) Bear with each other and (7) forgive whatever grievances you may have against one another. Forgive as the Lord forgave you.* **And over all these virtues (8) put on love, which binds them all together in perfect unity.** *(Col.3:12-14 NIV)*

Seven pearls of great value are joined together by a pure gold strand of love (charity). When we think of charity today, we often think of providing a meal for the poor, or helping victims of natural disasters with food, clothing, etc. And, yes, these are acts of charity; however, as we look at the Scriptures above we see charity involves changes in heart and temperament as well. Holiness and righteousness before God cannot be attained without the working of charity within our hearts. Charity, or agape love, as it is known, is best equated with a nurturing mother's love. When a child is sick, its mother doesn't simply provide a bowl of soup and a warm blanket and walk away. She remains with the child, comforting him, encouraging him to eat and take his medications, and assuring him that he will recover and be able to run and play again. She is showing love to her child which strengthens him in several ways.

In the early church, holiness and charity were inseparable doctrines, and they should be today. A man may think that because he abstained from evil, he was living a life of righteousness, but he would soon learn that without charity his abstention was for naught. Paul wrote to the Corinthian church this same message.

> *Though I speak with the tongues of men and of angels, and have not charity, I am become as sounding brass, or a tinkling cymbal. And though I have the gift of prophecy, and understand all mysteries, and all knowledge; and though I have all faith, so that I could remove mountains, and have not charity, I am nothing.* **And though I bestow all my goods to feed the**

poor, and though I give my body to be burned, and have not charity, it profiteth me nothing. Charity suffereth long, and is kind; charity envieth not; charity vaunteth not itself, is not puffed up, Doth not behave itself unseemly, seeketh not her own, is not easily provoked, thinketh no evil; Rejoiceth not in iniquity, but rejoiceth in the truth; Beareth all things, believeth all things, hopeth all things, endureth all things.
(I Cor.13:1-7)

Charity in the heart of a believer is truly a Light to attract the world. It is not haughty and neither does it brag about its successes, skills or intellect. Charity condescends to men of lesser skills and intellect, making allowances for their lack of understanding or expertise.

Without disciplining our temperament, how can we be long-suffering? Our human patience cannot come close to the patience required by charity. Without charity abiding in our hearts certain temperaments are impossible to change. How can we say we're *not easily provoked*, when the slightest insult triggers a vicious verbal or physical attack? *Think no evil, and endure all things?* Impossible! Without bringing down our self-pride how can we be *non-envious*, and refrain from boasting of our freedom from a certain entanglement, such as drugs and alcohol? Can you see yourself fulfilling a stranger's needs before providing for your own? Impossible! Without the power of God's Holy Spirit working in you to change your heart and mind, maybe you will give a beggar a dollar or two; and even that may be a struggle for some; but to fulfill all the characterizations of Godly charity? Impossible!

Charity is a cherished treasure that comes directly from the heart of God, from his Holy Spirit, to the one whose only hope and desire is to glorify the Father in Christ Jesus, our Lord; to the one who wants to walk in holiness and righteousness before him. It is the outward expression of the inner workings of Godly love, mercy, and grace combined that is given through Jesus Christ to be exercised with all diligence. For me to expound upon God's love, grace and mercy to the fullest extent the

Scriptures permit, I would find myself practically rewriting the Bible – not as a substitute – but to the magnificent glory of Almighty God. But take a moment to consider your answer to these questions: In our current state of mind, are we willing to lay our life on the altar of sacrifice to be perfected by the Lord for the sole benefit of others? That's what Jesus did. Are we willing to undergo the disciplines, fasting, and prayers necessary to be entrusted with charity for God's eternal glory? These are tough questions; but without the Spirit of charity working in our hearts and injecting its humility and temperance into our souls, the chances are great that this mind, which was in Christ Jesus, is not in us right now.

How can one testify that Christianity is the true faith when Christianity's God and his word are set aside and ignored? Instead of preaching prosperity, pastors and evangelists should be promoting God's word of walking in the Light of his salvation which includes a life of holiness, charity, and soberness of mind.

Are you willing to have others joining you in sincere prayer for the love of God that passes all understanding and enjoy the blessings and benefits that may be derived from your faith? Godly charity is a triune essence consisting of God's mercy, grace, and holiness. One cannot be separated from the other without altering its composition and perfection.

Yes, the mystery of charity includes the very essence of true mercy, grace, and holiness strengthened and established by faith. Faith is the anchor and generator of charity.

FAITH

Faith is one of the more profound mysteries of the Gospel. In (1Tim. 3:8,9) Paul speaks of the deacons holding the mystery of the faith in a pure conscience. In many places in the letters of Paul the word, "faith" can be transposed with the words, "Jesus Christ" without changing its meaning or context, for example: "Without faith [Jesus Christ] it is impossible to please God." (Heb. 11:6) However, in most places, faith is seen as the essence and gift that comes from the bosom of Christ Jesus.

In modern times, "faith" is often described as believing in something that can't be seen. For example; God cannot be seen but we believe he exists. But what is this type of faith based on – imagination, will, hypotheses, positive thinking, or truth?

Faith is always based on what is absolutely true, not merely believable. It is trust in the living word of God whereby the disciple believes the Lord's word and that whatsoever he says is destined to come to pass. But it must be the Lord's actual word in the context of how he meant it, not simply one's rendition or paraphrase which, more often than not, is denominationally slanted or void of truth altogether. The best answer to what faith encompasses can be found in the book of Hebrews.

> Now **faith is being sure** of what we hope for **and certain** of what we do not see. (Heb. 11:1 NIV)

Faith was considered a sacred treasure in the early church - given by God in incremental portions to those who were able to trust God's word and act upon it. It wasn't their imagination or positive thinking that brought results, but their trust in God's truthfulness and the acts of God's righteousness that followed. This was their definition of true faith.

Today's Christian may ask, "If we don't have this strong faith, how can one receive the gift of salvation? Aren't we saved by grace through faith?" First of all, no one receives Jesus Christ into their hearts because he has the faith to be saved. According to Jesus no one comes to him of their own volition; the Father literally drags him to the cross. *(John 5:44)* The messenger preaches the Gospel and literally persuades the unbeliever to "Hope" in the truth of his message. This is the hope Paul referred to in his epistle to the Romans. *(Rom. 8:24,25)* And, *"Now the God of hope fill you with all joy and peace in believing, that ye may abound in hope, through the power of the Holy Ghost."* *(Rom 15:13)*

Consider this analogy: You are a man heavily in debt and see no way out of your predicament. A friend of yours knows of your dilemma and offers to help you out of your difficulty. He offers to lead you to a benefactor who can help. You don't know this benefactor and are skeptical of his willingness to help, but at the same time, your heart is filled with hope the man will come through for you. To your surprise he offers to help and you readily accept the man's offer. Now you wait with anxious hope that he won't renege on his promise. Once the promise is fulfilled, you acknowledge the benefactor's credibility and your heart is filled with gratitude. So it is with everyone who hears the Gospel but has no personal knowledge of Jesus Christ. The Lord never fails to fulfill the hope of the one "submitting" to the words of the preacher as long as his message is based on truth rather than opinion. If the Lord does not fulfill the preacher's word, don't blame the Lord; find another preacher. Faith is measured, beginning with hope and fulfilled in absolute assurance.

Hope, the most simplistic faith, is the beginning of an unbeliever's trust in the Word of Truth. The Lord transforms, little by little, this meager hope into an enduring confidence: giving credence to one of the meanings of the phrase, *from faith to faith*. This is the faith the apostles prayed for and shared with one another for the edification of the church body. It is this confidence, this sweet assurance that is imputed to man as a sacred responsibility, even the faith of Abraham the disciples often referred to. This sacred faith which has the power to move mountains, separate the seas, call down fire from heaven, love an enemy, and heal the sick, is measured out to everyone, along with faith's conjoined partner, *Righteousness*. This is the shield of faith given to the Soldiers and Sons of Light with which they are able to ward off all the fiery darts of the wicked.

> *Then came the disciples to Jesus apart, and said, Why could not we cast him out? And Jesus said unto them, Because of your unbelief: for verily I say unto you, if ye have faith as a grain of mustard seed, ye shall say unto this mountain, Remove hence to yonder place; and it shall remove; and **nothing shall be impossible unto you**.* (Mat 17:19,20)

This is the true faith through which Jesus and the disciples worked miracles. With this kind of faith nothing is impossible. It is said that faith is believing the things that are unseen yet considered valid. I have to ask this question: Who determines the validity of something unseen? How is it confirmed? Again, true faith is not based on imagination, lofty ideals, or carefully devised fables. It is written: *for the imagination of man's heart is evil from his youth;* (Gen. 8:21). In fact, in every place in the Scriptures where the word "imagination" is found, it is denigrated. This being written, why would God want us to have faith based on our imagination and hypotheticals?

God and truth are identifiable by certain unmistakable proofs. It is fair to say that belief in an imaginary god is no different than believing in a false god because neither one speaks to us. If God had but one disparaging remark to make toward the ministry, it would be their insistence the people "accept by faith" [imagination] the doctrines they teach without having to submit proofs of their truthfulness. For this reason, millions of people have given up on the Christian faith because the god they were taught to believe in didn't answer their prayers. To everyone I make the following promise: If you will turn your eyes toward the sky and call out to the Father in heaven and pray words like these; "Holy Father in heaven, I don't know you, but I want to know. I don't want to believe in something or someone who doesn't exist, or is a counterfeit; I want to know you. Will you reveal yourself to me in a way that I can relate to your reality and may believe what is true?"

I assure you that God will make himself known to you so that your faith is based on truth, not imagination. I did this, and I have told countless numbers of people to do the same thing, and God has never disappointed any of us. I have never met a Christian who didn't have "faith". Yet, for all the alleged faith that exists around the world, the Lord asked this question. *Nevertheless when the Son of man cometh, shall he find faith on the earth?* (Luke 18:8)

I can't help but wonder if this same thinking went into this admonition by Paul to the Corinthian church:

> *Examine yourselves, whether ye be in the faith;[in Christ] prove your own selves. Know ye not your own selves, how that Jesus Christ is in you, except ye be reprobates?* [fail the test?] (2 Cor 13:5)

The Father only wants men and women to serve him with a trusting heart and devotion; not as mere robots yielding to religious mandates. This type of faith is what Abraham, the prophets, Jesus, and the disciples all testified of. They knew in advance what fate awaited them and they approached it with the confidence that if death was required, God was able and willing to resurrect them again. God provided a goat to be sacrificed in place of Isaac. He allowed Daniel to escape the teeth of the lions; and He raised Jesus from the grave. Each one found themselves in an undesirable place, but yielded to the will of the Father.

Only by the transformation and renewing of our minds do we find ourselves in a Spiritual position to prove what the perfect will of God is so that we never need to be found lacking and ashamed.

> _For I say_, through the grace given unto me, _to every man that is among you, not to think of himself more highly than he ought to think_; but to _think soberly_, according **as God hath dealt to every man the measure of faith**. For as we have many members in one body, and all members have not the same office: _So we_, being many, _are one body in Christ_, and every one members one of another. Having then gifts differing according to the grace that is given to us, whether _prophecy, let us prophesy according to the proportion of faith_; Or _ministry, let us_

wait on our ministering: or he that teacheth, on teaching; Or he that exhorteth, on exhortation: he that giveth, let him do it with simplicity; he that ruleth, with diligence; he that showeth mercy, with cheerfulness. Let love be without dissimulation [pretention]. ***Abhor that which is evil; cleave to that which is good. Be kindly affectioned one to another with brotherly love;*** *in honour preferring one another; Not slothful in business; fervent in spirit; serving the Lord; Rejoicing in hope; patient in tribulation; continuing instant in prayer; Distributing to the necessity of saints; given to hospitality. Bless them which persecute you: bless, and curse not. Rejoice with them that do rejoice, and weep with them that weep.* ***Be of the same mind one toward another.*** *Mind not high things, but condescend to men of low estate. Be not wise in your own conceits. Recompense to no man evil for evil. Provide things honest in the sight of all men.* ***If it be possible, as much as lieth in you, live peaceably with all men.*** *Dearly beloved, avenge not yourselves, but rather give place unto wrath: for it is written, Vengeance is mine; I will repay, saith the Lord. Therefore if thine enemy hunger, feed him; if he thirst, give him drink: for in so doing thou shalt* *heap coals of fire on his head. <u>Be not</u>* *<u>overcome of evil, but overcome evil with</u>* *<u>good.</u>* *(Rom 12:1-21)*

This laundry list of responsibilities reveals the actual work of faith, gushing through the righteousness given to us by the wholesomeness of Almighty God who entrusts us with this sacred treasure. These responsibilities are not to be taken lightly, or be excused when we fail to perform them. These are the works of faith that should cause us to mourn in the spirit when we fail. The essence of Godly faith is hope, love, and trust. I can write volumes on true faith; but, if one claims to be a believer in Christ and cannot testify of the hope he has in Christ Jesus, his faith is irrelevant and spiritless. How then can this person please God?

Many religions speak of faith [blind faith] acquired from their holy books, prophets, and even imaginary beings; but true Christian faith speaks of faith as proofs and evidence of things unseen; things that are confirmed by our Lord as truth.

The mystery of faith is first revealed by the newly discovered "hope" in the Word of God that fills a void in the new prospective believer. Then, faith slowly but surely evolves into an enduring confidence and trust in the Father through Jesus Christ, our Lord. The ultimate faith knows no bounds, but is ever working to bring glory, honor, and praise to the Most High God in Christ Jesus.

Knowing in advance that your faith will be tested, have the courage to open your heart and ask the Lord to continuously increase your faith (your trust in him). He will gladly oblige.

RIGHTEOUSNESS

Isn't righteousness the same as being charitable? Righteousness is a conjoined partner with charity, and therefore has its own unique identity as well. Righteousness in the heart of a person will cause him to perform many charitable deeds, but righteousness demands one more virtue.

Righteousness is putting the cares, needs, and cries for help from others before your own. For example: Let's say you have $1,000 dollars for your rent which is due tomorrow. But today, a friend of yours reveals that his sister needs $1,000 today or the loan company is going to take her car which she desperately needs to get to work and take her sickly child to the doctor. It is not uncommon to have a thought saying, "How will I pay my rent tomorrow?" But have you learned the word of God regarding this opportunity? If so, He will bring them to mind:

> *He that hath pity upon the poor lendeth unto the LORD; and that which he hath given will he pay him again.*
> *(Prov 19:17)*

In other words, you are instructed to satisfy the needs of the poor today with your substance, and trust that God will make sure you are not lacking anything. Your rent will surely be paid. This act of righteousness requires two of God's gifts; faith, and charity which you have already decided to give of yourself to the Lord.

Among the many Christian doctrines that are argued passionately, it is righteousness. Since the righteousness of the Lord is characterized by many in a false light, I am devoting a short chapter to its properties. Is it a characterization of God? Does it lie within the bosom of the Father? Does he "impute" his righteousness to another? Since the answer to each of these questions is "yes", then righteousness is a sacred paragon of virtue resting in the bosom of the Father, and one that God vests in those who are committed to a deep faith in him.

This is one of the more difficult mysteries to disclose, along with faith, because we all come to the altar of God with our own definition of righteousness, and we fail so miserably time and again to fulfill its precepts because of our preconceptions and personal needs.

In the book of Job as well as Paul's epistle, we are given an example of faulty viewpoints on righteousness:

> Then answered Bildad the Shuhite, and said, How long wilt thou speak these things? and how long shall the words of thy mouth be like a strong wind? Doth God pervert judgment? or doth the Almighty pervert justice? If thy children have sinned against him, and he have cast them away for their transgression; If thou wouldest seek unto God betimes, and make thy supplication to the Almighty; **If thou wert pure and upright; surely now he would awake for thee, and make the habitation of thy righteousness prosperous.** Though thy beginning was small, yet thy latter end should greatly increase. (Job 8:7)

Generally speaking, this is the doctrine most commonly used in the modern church. Worshippers are taught that righteousness is walking uprightly, so that others may see your good works and glorify the Father in heaven; a doctrine that is true in part.

What then shall we say? That the Gentiles, who did not pursue righteousness, have obtained it, a righteousness that is by faith; but Israel, who pursued a law of righteousness, has not attained it. Why not? **Because they pursued it not by faith but as if it were by works.** *They stumbled over the "stumbling stone." As it is written:* **"See, I lay in Zion a stone that causes men to stumble and a rock that makes them fall,** *and the one who trusts in him will never be put to shame."* (Rom 9:30-33 NIV)

This is the faith we bring to the table. We "believe" that if we obey the commandments that tell us what we must do; and, obey those that tell us what not to do, our righteousness will be favorable in the eyes of the Lord. There is certainly nothing wrong with living "according to the rules of obedience", as long as we understand this is "righteousness" according to the Mt. Sinai covenant, the Law of Moses; that it is not "righteousness" according to the law of the Spirit in Christ Jesus. And, like I said, we've all accepted this "doctrine" at some point in our lives and have fallen into a depressed state of mind when we come to the realization that it is literally impossible to keep every commandment of the law.

When we reach this mental state we are often comforted with a statement such as: *There is no condemnation to those who are in Christ Jesus.* Unfortunately, this verse is often received as a license to continue in sin. Nevertheless, it is not impossible to obey every inclination of the Spirit.

We tithe; we perform many other works of righteousness: the question is why—out of the new freewill nature created in us—or because we're being obedient and hoping for a hundred fold reward? Which heart do you think is most acceptable to the Lord?

To use an analogy, righteousness is the glove, faith is the hand, and charity is the power that moves the hand and brings attention to the glove. Hence, the works of righteousness accomplished through the Spirit of Christ are visible to the naked eye, whereas its source and influences are only visible to those with the gift of discernment.

*For I say unto you, that **except your righteousness shall exceed the righteousness of the scribes and Pharisees, ye shall in no case enter into the kingdom of heaven.*** (Mat 5:20)

Therefore no one will be declared righteous in his sight by observing the law; *rather, through the law we become conscious of sin.* ***But now a righteousness from God, apart from law, has been made known, to which the Law and the Prophets testify. This righteousness from God comes through faith in Jesus Christ to all who believe.***
(Rom 3:20-22 NIV)

Our own righteousness is as filthy rags in his sight, but the righteousness that comes through faith in Christ Jesus our Lord, is precious to him. Obedience to the Law is good; but only in Christianity can we be obedient to the law of the Spirit that is in Christ who dwells in us.

What does God want from us? A heart that yields to His urging and filled with the faith that he cannot speak an untruth and will surely repay what we give to the poor. Are we willing to surrender our heart and pray for the faith to work His righteousness among the lost and needy? The next set of disciplines will require absolute loyalty, a more mature faith, love of charity, righteousness, and holiness. If we are lacking in any one of these areas of spiritual growth we simply need to go back and concentrate on embracing the previous disciplines. It is God's will that we achieve the highest levels of spiritual development. As previously noted, the disciplines of God are progressive, one precious stone set upon another. So don't be disheartened if you must spend more time developing your faith, holiness and righteousness.

WISDOM

Wisdom is one of the greatest mysteries that is impossible to unravel apart from having a close-knit relationship with Jesus Christ so that he can impart his wisdom, understanding and knowledge to every one of us. This is his perfect will. It is written:

> *Whom shall he teach knowledge? and whom shall he make to understand doctrine? them that are weaned from the milk, and drawn from the breasts.* ***For precept must be upon precept, precept upon precept; line upon line, line upon line; here a little, and there a little:*** *(Isa 28:9,10)*

Wisdom preserves the sanctity of all hidden truths and the mysteries of the kingdom, which are ultimately made known to us by the spirit of prophecy. Wisdom acts as the shield, the insulator of truth; and truth, like a strand of pure gold, runs through and connects the pearls of wisdom together. Although the essence of truth is integrated in the depths of wisdom, it is revealed and exposed by the graces that wisdom illuminates. Wisdom is given to glorify and magnify the persona of the True God; for without wisdom, truth remains unseen and unheard. Therefore, wisdom is the primary gift to be much desired.

> See, I have taught you decrees and laws as the LORD my God commanded me, so that you may follow them in the land you are entering to take possession of it. **Observe them carefully, for this will show your wisdom and understanding to the nations, who will hear about all these decrees and say, "Surely this great nation is a wise and understanding people."** What other nation is so great as to have their gods near them the way the LORD our God is near us whenever we pray to him? And what other nation is so great as to have such righteous decrees and laws as this body of laws I am setting before you today? Only be careful, and watch yourselves closely so that you do not forget the things your eyes have seen or let them slip from your heart as long as you live. Teach them to your children and to their children after them. (Deu 4:5-9)
>
> **The proverbs of Solomon** son of David, king of Israel: **for attaining wisdom and discipline; for understanding words of**

insight; for acquiring a disciplined and prudent life, doing what is right and just and fair; for giving prudence to the simple, knowledge and discretion to the young--let the wise listen and add to their learning, and let the discerning get guidance--for understanding proverbs and parables, the sayings and riddles of the wise. (Prov. 1: 1-6 NIV)

Solomon tells us that Wisdom is the disciplinarian, the teacher of justice, equity, and every good path of righteousness. Without Godly righteousness, wisdom, truth, faith and holiness remain hidden from the eyes of unbelievers and believers alike.

Wisdom, and the practice of wisdom, far excels wise axioms and the unraveling of riddles and dark sayings. While wisdom is the principal way to truth; knowledge and understanding are the pathways to wisdom. Wisdom presents itself after three distinct events take place in our hearts. First, we become aware of, and gain knowledge of God; then we get an understanding of his creativity, his methods, and his will, answering the questions of why, how, what, etc.; and lastly, prudence dictates the time and place such understanding may be revealed. This is how wisdom reveals itself. **Before wisdom is revealed in the heart, the soul must have a fear of the Lord [which only the Lord can give]; faith, knowledge, and understanding of Godliness, the righteousness and holiness of God, and the confidence that He cannot lie or deceive — all the pearls we have looked at thus far.**

> *I, wisdom, dwell with prudence, and find out knowledge of witty inventions [mischievous intentions]. **The fear of the LORD is to hate evil: pride,** and **arrogancy,** and **the evil way,** and **the froward mouth,** do I hate. Counsel is mine, and sound wisdom: I am understanding; I have strength. By me kings reign, and princes decree justice. By me princes rule, and nobles, even all the judges of the earth. **I love them that love me; and those that seek me early shall find me.*** (Prov 8:12-17)

> **For the LORD gives wisdom, and from his mouth comes knowledge and understanding.** *He holds victory in store for the upright, he is a shield to those whose walk is blameless, **for he***

*guards the course of the just and
protects the way of his faithful ones.*
(Prov. 2:6-8 NIV)

Wisdom is the gift that opens the perception
of the believer causing him to discern the thoughts
and intents of someone's heart. Discernment and
discretion saves the wise in heart from the evil
intentions of his fellow man.

> *Then you will understand what is
> right and just and fair--every good
> path. For wisdom will enter your heart,
> and knowledge will be pleasant to your
> soul. Discretion will protect you, and
> understanding will guard you.
> Wisdom will save you from the ways
> of wicked men, from men whose
> words are perverse, who leave the
> straight paths to walk in dark ways,
> who delight in doing wrong and rejoice
> in the perverseness of evil, whose
> paths are crooked and who are devious
> in their ways. It will save you also
> from the adulteress, from the
> wayward wife with her seductive
> words, who has left the partner of her
> youth and ignored the covenant she
> made before God. (Prov 2:9-17 NIV)*

The beauty of wisdom is a delight to those who have it. Through wisdom, a leader is able to make sound decisions that will bring prosperity and peace to his people. It is obvious to all that he is caring, loving, just, and supportive of equality, justice, and every good and honest endeavor. Through wisdom, he is capable of sound leadership and creative problem solving. Wisdom surrounds himself with others of like mind who are both prudent and discerning.

The foolish leader is quite the opposite. His decisions are void of charity, love, and equity. He panders to those who are void of wisdom and surrounds himself with those like himself. In his days, peace, security, and stability are withheld from the people, and he laughs at the sound of their cries. He despises wisdom because wisdom reveals to the world that his ways are self-serving and evil. He is incapable of godly leadership and is void of creative thought. All his ways reveal his foolishness.

Pure wisdom can be compared to the secret place of the Most High. He shows his love by protecting the one who loves him, and teaches him how to walk in justice and equity.

> O ye simple, understand wisdom: and, ye fools, be ye of an understanding heart. Hear; for I will speak of excellent things; and the opening of my lips shall be right things. **For my mouth shall speak truth**; and wickedness is an abomination to my lips. **All the words of my mouth are in righteousness**; there is nothing froward or perverse in them. They are all plain to him that understandeth, and right to them that find knowledge. (Prov. 8:5-9)

To be trusted with the gift of wisdom one must be trained and disciplined in its arts. Many fiery trials and disciplines are involved in the instruction of Wisdom and hidden truths. The Lord makes you aware of wisdom's inestimable value, which we must never diminish.

> But **where shall wisdom be found?** and **where is the place of understanding**? Man knoweth not the price thereof; **neither is it found in the land of the living. The depth saith, It is not in me: and the sea saith, It is not with me.** It cannot be gotten for gold, neither shall silver be weighed for the price

thereof. It cannot be valued with the gold of Ophir, with the precious onyx, or the sapphire. The gold and the crystal cannot equal it: and the exchange of it shall not be for jewels of fine gold. No mention shall be made of coral, or of pearls: **for the price of wisdom is above rubies. The topaz of Ethiopia shall not equal it, neither shall it be valued with pure gold. Whence then cometh wisdom**? *and where is the place of understanding? Seeing it is hid from the eyes of all living, and kept close from the fowls of the air. Destruction and death say, We have heard the fame thereof with our ears.* **God understandeth the way thereof, and he knoweth the place thereof.** *For he looketh to the ends of the earth, and seeth under the whole heaven; To make the weight for the winds; and he weigheth the waters by measure. When he made a decree for the rain, and a way for the lightning of the thunder: Then did he see it, and declare it; he prepared it, yea, and searched it out.* **And unto man he said, Behold, the fear of the Lord, that is wisdom; and to depart from evil is understanding.** *(Job 28:12-28)*

Where is wisdom found? It is found in the heart of a wise man that has developed a deep respect and honor for the Lord. Where is the wise man, in the depth of the sea; in the heart of the abyss? No, he is hiding in the secret place of the Most High God learning the arts of wisdom and truth from his lips.

THE VALUE OF WISDOM

My son, let not them depart from thine eyes: **keep sound wisdom and discretion:** *So shall they be life unto thy soul, and grace to thy neck.* **Then shalt thou walk in thy way safely, and thy foot shall not stumble.** *When thou liest down, thou shalt not be afraid: yea, thou shalt lie down, and thy sleep shall be sweet.* (Prov 3:21-24)

<u>Wisdom is supreme; therefore get wisdom</u>. **Though it cost all you have,** [friends, family, and fortune] **get understanding. Esteem her, and she will exalt you; embrace her, and she will honor you.** (Prov 4:7,8)

The value of Wisdom is infinite particularly since it is an accumulation of doctrines that reveal the righteousness, will, justice, and judgments of Almighty God. Wisdom reveals the Peace that passes all understanding, the nurturing type of love that comes from the Father and his awesome heart of mercy, forgiveness and grace.

Wisdom is also a trinity in its consistency: knowledge, understanding, and prudence comprise its essence. To have one or two parts of Wisdom's essential core without the third part blocks the discovery of truth. Hopefully, you are beginning to see why these virtues of Christ Jesus must be desired with your whole heart and soul, and cherished for the holiness and presence of God that is revealed in them.

If the world was to witness men and women with wisdom, there would be little doubt that Christianity is the true faith. There are those who are considered wise by virtue of their education in worldly wisdom, but the wisdom that comes from God is unavailable to those who do not seek his kingdom and righteousness through the Holy Spirit.

To acquire wisdom we must be willing to enter into the secret place of the Most High God and dwell within the Light —the place where hope, faith, charity, faith, righteousness and salvation takes on an entirely new meaning—abiding in the vine as a fruitful branch that bears much fruit for the glory of God. Understand this; there are many who may not be willing to surrender all to acquire wisdom. Wisdom is not essential for one's salvation; however, for those who seek a higher position in ministry wisdom is to be much desired. This is what God wants from all of his ministers—to uncover the depths of truth, obtaining wisdom is paramount.

TRUTH – the Sword of the Spirit

In the early church, the mystery of truth had a much different meaning then it does today. Truth was more than mere words; it was a trinity consisting of the person, power, and virtues of Almighty God in action.

The qualitative essence of truth can be likened to the characteristics of the sun. Light rays are invisible to the naked eye; yet, they have perceptible features that enable us to discern, identify, and definitively confirm their reality, power (energy), and benefits. And, like the rays emanating from the sun, it is impossible for the earth to fully absorb, to the exclusion of all other heavenly bodies, the massive volume of energy and light it produces. Similarly, it isn't possible for one human being or religious group to absorb the fullness of "truth" to the exclusion of all others.

The concept that truth is invisible to the naked eye defies some rational thought, but so does the assertion that truth has the attributes of a living personality, namely, God. This was a concept endorsed by Jesus of Nazareth and his disciples. How did they support this "belief"? They expanded the characteristics of truth by alleging that the essence of truth; that it actually possesses an invisible living persona, a conscious nature.

John, an early Church father wrote: *"...And it is the Spirit that beareth witness, because the Spirit is truth.* (1 John 5.6) He referred to truth as a Living Spirit capable of testifying. An authentic witness is described as an individual who demonstrates his capacity to rationalize, remember critical details, recall information from memory; and then testify to their certainty. His statements are examined and every attempt is made to uncover any inaccuracies or inconsistencies: if none are found, his testimony is considered credible. So it is with God's holy Word.

Jesus of Nazareth also testified that truth had a distinct persona. In one such example, he spoke of himself, saying, *"I am ... the Truth."* (John 14.6) And in another place, he gave this teaching: *"Howbeit when **he**, the Spirit of truth, is come, **he** will guide you into all truth: for **he** shall not speak of **himself**; but* *whatsoever **he** shall hear, that shall **he** speak: and **he** will show you things to come."* (John 16.13)

In these statements, Jesus clearly gives truth the qualitative essence of a living, conscious personality—a persona with the ability to reason, educate, guide, and reveal truths. I came to learn that Truth is the essence and convincing confirmation, the proof, that the distinguished persona of the Spirit of God is present when truth is spoken; that His presence is manifested by his words—words that typify a loving and gentle graciousness, a nurturing love, with an unadulterated perfection that can't be contradicted or overwhelmed. Truth is Jesus Christ personified.

As previously written, truth is hidden within wisdom and is available to those who would abide in Christ and seek the truths of the Lord with all their heart. The catechist ordained for the ministry was instructed in ways that made their soul crave truth and its mysteries. And while truth must be diligently searched for, there were several disciplines they had to learn in order to recognize it. Because of the many tricks of the adversary, they needed to be taught how to validate what they had discovered was, in fact, the truth. There is an interesting example of discerning the fullness of truth given to us in the book of Acts.

> *Meanwhile a Jew named Apollos, a native of Alexandria, came to Ephesus. He was a learned man, with a thorough knowledge of the Scriptures. He had been instructed in the way of the Lord, and he spoke with great fervor and taught about Jesus accurately, though he knew only the baptism of John. He began to speak boldly in the synagogue. When Priscilla and Aquila heard him, they invited him to their home and explained to him the way of God more adequately. For he mightily convinced the Jews, and that publicly, showing by the scriptures that Jesus was Christ.* (Acts 18:24-26, 28 NIV)

Through his teaching many received Christ as their Savior. Nevertheless, something was missing which Priscilla and Aquila were able to discern. They felt compelled to take the Billy Graham of his day aside, and explain the way of God more perfectly to him. Now if he spoke about Jesus accurately and boldly, showing that he was the Christ and converting the Jews, what could he possibly be missing? By the way, he was also credited with starting a school of ministry in Ephesus.

> *And it came to pass, that, while Apollos was at Corinth, Paul having passed through the upper coasts came to Ephesus: and finding certain disciples, He said unto them, Have ye received the Holy Ghost since ye believed? And they said unto him, We have not so much as heard whether there be any Holy Ghost. And he said unto them, Unto what then were ye baptized? And they said, Unto John's baptism. Then said Paul, John verily baptized with the baptism of repentance, saying unto the people, that they should believe on him which should come after him, that is, on Christ Jesus. When they heard this, they were baptized in the name of the Lord Jesus. And when Paul had laid his hands upon them, the Holy Ghost came on them; and they spake with tongues, and prophesied. And all the men were about twelve.* (Acts 19:1-7 NIV)

This time it was Paul who came upon Apollos' disciples; he listened to them and found something amiss. Was it merely the fact they had not been baptized in the name of Jesus Christ? Would water baptism have changed their teaching? No; but when Paul laid hands upon them and began to pray, the Holy Spirit came upon them and they witnessed the Lord's presence by glorifying God in a heavenly tongue. Having stated the obvious, we still don't have an answer yet as to what Apollos was lacking. Did Priscilla and Aquila pray for him to receive the baptism in Christ and in the Holy Spirit? It isn't written and I highly doubt it because he didn't share the experience with his disciples.

Apollos was able to preach Jesus Christ and him crucified, but, the one thing he failed to disclose was that all the works fulfilled by Christ were executed by the Father in him. Therefore, **his message lacked the one part that is essential in the discovery of truth – the Father must be glorified in the Son**. This was the missing element that Priscilla, Aquila, and Paul were able to discern from Apollos' teaching. Truth in itself must glorify and personify the holiness and majesty of the Father and the works he accomplished in Christ beginning at a time before the foundation of the world was laid.

Today, it is often said, "The Scriptures are the Word of God". This statement leaves a false impression with many and therefore must be addressed. Standing alone, it leads one to believe, or assume, that whenever someone, especially a minister, reads from or quotes from the Holy Scriptures he is speaking the truth. Now, most of us know that isn't a valid statement at all. In the Gospel of Luke we find the Tempter quoting from Psalm 91 as he tried to entice Jesus. Yes, even the devil can quote the Scriptures and read from the Bible.

Truth is the Word of God without question to the one whose eyes have been opened. Truth is the personification of the Lord Jesus, and truth is identified as the Word of God as you would hear it flow from the Lord's own lips if he opened your ears to hear his voice. Truth must glorify the great mystery of the Gospel, or it isn't truth. There are many religions which elevate books they consider equal to, or of greater importance than the Holy

Gospel and its mystery of salvation. The question is whether these "other books" ever bring honor and glory to the Father in Jesus Christ. As we have seen, the mystery of the Gospel is the shed light, the life blood of God, being poured out upon all flesh, lighting every child that comes into the world, and making a way for every willing soul to walk in his Light. If this book bore witness to the truth, it must include this great lesson whereby we declare the love of God for all mankind as it is revealed in the Gospel.

Truth creates in us a resolute faith in the holiness, faithfulness and merciful ways of God; and enables us to "know" in the deepest part of our soul that God means what he says, and pours out his Love upon us for the salvation of our souls. As an example, Jesus taught his disciples:

> *And as Moses lifted up the serpent in the wilderness, even so must the Son of man be lifted up: That whosoever believeth in him should not perish, but have eternal life. **For God so loved the world, that he gave his only begotten Son, that whosoever believeth in him should not perish, but have everlasting life.** For God sent not his Son into*

*the world to condemn the world; but that the world through him might be saved. **He that believeth on him is not condemned: but he that believeth not is condemned already**, because he hath not **believed in the name** of the only begotten Son of God."* (Jn.3:14-18)

Notice how Jesus preached the works of the Father and glorified him in his teachings. All of the disciples who were educated in truth also bore witness of the Father's love in Christ Jesus.

Believing in the *name* refers to God's renown, his reputation, and the accounts of his mighty deeds of deliverance, forgiveness, mercy, honor, and faithfulness to name a few. Truth gives us a deep inner "knowing" that he is the pure Light of the world that draws those that seek him unto himself; those who worship and love him, not out of obligation to the commands in the Law, but out of a free-will Spirit, motivated by love and devotion. This is what the newer converts were taught in the first century:

And this is the condemnation, that light is come into the world, and men loved darkness rather than light, because their deeds were evil. For every one that doeth evil hateth the light, neither cometh to the light, lest his deeds should be reproved. But *he that doeth truth cometh to the light, that his deeds may be made manifest, that they are wrought in God.* (John 3:19-21)

But the hour cometh, and now is, when the true worshippers shall worship the Father in spirit and in truth: for the Father seeketh such to worship him. God is a Spirit: and they that worship him must worship him in spirit and in truth. (John 4:23-24)

In conjunction with the Gospel, the disciples learned that truth and wisdom draws the servant of God into a fulfilling relationship with the Lord. And by abiding in him we are able to **receive counsel at his lips**, **learn his ways**, his methods, and **experience his great love for us**. Unless we abide in him, God will not reveal his truth to us. Think about it; when a deep, undying love engulfs your heart for a member of the opposite sex, is anything less than an intimate relationship truly satisfying? Jesus and John the Younger taught their disciples the following lessons:

> *Then said Jesus to those Jews which believed on him,* **If ye continue [abide] in my word, then are ye my disciples indeed; And ye shall know the truth,** *and the truth shall make you free.* (John 8:31,32 NIV)

> *And this is the promise that he hath promised us, even eternal life. These things have I written unto you concerning them that seduce you.* **But <u>the anointing</u> which ye have received of him <u>abideth in you</u>, and <u>ye need not that any man teach you</u>: but as <u>the same anointing teacheth you</u> of all things, <u>and is truth</u>, and is no lie, and even as it hath taught you, <u>ye shall abide in him</u>.**
> (1 Jn.2:26,27)

> <u>***And now, little children, abide in him***</u>; *that, when he shall appear, we may have confidence, and not be ashamed before him at his coming. If ye know that he is righteous, ye know that every one that doeth righteousness is born of him.* (1 John 2:28-29)

As we abide in the Father, we abide in the truth, which is Christ, and in his glorious light where all his gifts, blessings, and sacred trusts can be found.

Prayer is instantaneous to the point we can barely contain ourselves in our praises of God. The joy of the Lord and his words of love will burst off the lips of those who are intimate with him.

You will be able to respond to, and trust in, the Voice of the Lord of Hosts, and only his voice. **Knowing**, not merely *believing*, but **knowing** the voice of the Lord is the only way you will see the victories of truth unfold. For where the word of the Lord is, his power is manifested.

Here is a lesson in truth of grave importance; and one we should all be aware of. Everyone, whether we realize it or not, is given the choice of which tree [which messenger] we will eat from, and whose words we will feed our souls with—the tree [messenger] of life, or the tree [messenger] of knowledge. In much the same way, we all face the same dilemma Adam was challenged with in the Garden of Eden. He was tempted to risk his eternal life, put his soul on the gambling table set before him, and make his wager, [I'm speaking figuratively, of course]. The stakes were very high; and he had to wager all that he had, his life, wife, his future seed, and the scepter of sovereign rule over the earth, on *what he was led to believe was truth* – that of him becoming like God. What were his choices? He could believe the words of his wife [or the serpent] or, he could believe the words of the True God [that he was ordained to rule over all the earth forever.] Was he forced to gamble? No; he only needed to call out to the Living God and ask him to confirm his word. The Lord would have rebuked the enemy of Adam's soul and rescued him from death. As it is written, *"Whosoever calls upon the name of the Lord will be saved* [rescued]." We all know the story: Adam decided to gamble everything on what he "chose to believe" or, "wanted to believe," and lost. This is what all of us need to learn—**we don't need to gamble**—the ear of the Lord is very near us, even at our lips, so there is no reason not to call upon him.

God forbid any of us should be found denying one his eternal salvation by asking him to accept our opinions or beliefs as the truth! I couldn't, and besides that, I don't have the fearlessness to be so reckless; and neither will you as you rest in the Lord.

To say there is "One Truth" is only valid if we are referring to the Father of Lights; and to have access to his truth, we must abide in him and he must remain in us. There is no other way, and only Christianity brings this truth to light.

What does God want from his ministry? He wants us to realize that truth is more than simple words or Bible verses. He wants us to seek the word as it proceeds from the lips of the Father in Christ Jesus. The question we have to answer is this: Are we willing to surrender all, if necessary, to abide in Him, giving up all other desires in the flesh in exchange for the anointed word that proceeds from the Lord?

PROPHECY

Does God want us to be prophets? *Is it possible to become a prophet of the Lord today?*

> *And Moses said unto him, Enviest thou for my sake?* **would God that all the LORD'S people were prophets, and that the LORD would put his spirit upon them!** *(Num 11:29)*

> *Follow after charity, and desire spiritual gifts, but rather that ye may prophesy. For he that speaketh in an unknown tongue speaketh not unto men, but unto God: for no man understandeth him; howbeit in the spirit he speaketh mysteries.* **But he that prophesieth speaketh unto men to edification, and exhortation, and comfort.** *He that speaketh in an unknown tongue edifieth himself; but* **he that prophesieth edifieth the church.** *I would that ye all spake with tongues, but rather that ye prophesied: for greater is he that prophesieth than he that speaketh with tongues, except he interpret, that the church may receive edifying. (1 Cor 14:1-5)*

Many believe that prophecy is the foretelling of future events, and while there is a sliver of truth mixed in with that statement, the massive amount of information attributed to prophecy is given little attention. I can say this with all certainty; learning the mysteries of prophecy is truly discipline under fire, intense fire. Why so? Because, by virtue of this gift we are not only given the ability to recognize the authentic Jesus, but to identify him, and testify of him in truth. The enemy uses every form of deception and flattery in its attempt to imitate the real Jesus Christ and deceives many. For the minister entrusted with the Lord's children, it is of paramount importance that he knows the difference between the true shepherd and gospel from fraudulent imitations.

Is this the work of the Lord? Yes, of course it is. The name, person, and power contained in the name of Jesus Christ, the true Son of the true God, sends tremors through the hearts of principalities, dominions and thrones adverse to the truth. There is one thing the powers of darkness do not want someone to do and that is to identify with and testify of, the Lord Jesus Christ in truth. It seemed like every power in Hell was sent my way to force me to quit, to give up under the strain, and content myself with saying what everyone is comfortable hearing; for which cause I can say, only by the grace of Almighty God working his will in me through Christ Jesus was I able to overcome and regain my focus.

And I could go on and speak of the trials and tribulations of Paul and Stephen, and others whose lives were in constant peril because of the testimony they held and were willing to give their lives for. Beyond any shadow of a doubt, the testimony of Jesus Christ is the power of Salvation to every soul under the heaven of heavens; and only in Christianity can this truth be discovered. Be assured that the power of salvation is met with tremendous force by the spirits of darkness.

What is the reward? That of knowing him and being able to discern his presence even in the worst of situations; having an inner peace that all will turn out well despite how they appear on the surface, and being able to share this confidence with those who are gripped with fear. This is how the church is edified through prophecy, and this is how many unbelievers are brought to the throne and given the gift of salvation.

Believing in the person and the history of Jesus Christ is good, but a faithful witness it does not make. Prophecy is the work of God, for the glory of the Son, and with the strength of the Spirit.

The apostles and prophets of old were well prepared for the obstacles they would face, having endured the most intense afflictions; and many failed, finding it much easier to prophesy by the spirit of devils rather than yield to the teachings of God. Search the Scriptures to find out their end. Why is prophecy of such enormous value? The reason is summed up in this one verse:

> And I fell at his feet to worship him. And he said unto me, See thou do it not: I am thy fellow servant, and of thy brethren that have the testimony of Jesus: worship God: **for the testimony of Jesus is the spirit of prophecy.**
> (Rev 19:10)

The testimony of Jesus Christ, being the Spirit of prophecy, must be one hundred percent truthful. There is no room for opinions and imaginary distortions. We can only preach those things that we know, have seen, or touched. The Lord doesn't need testimonies based on hearsay, opinion, commentary, or denominational indoctrination. He is Truth, and his witnesses must be the servants of Truth in order to bear true witness of him. John, the brother of Jesus, testified of this truth when he penned these words:

> ***That which was from the beginning,*** *which* **we have heard,** *which* **we have seen with our eyes,** *which* **we have looked upon,** *and* **our hands have handled, of the Word of life***; (For the life was manifested, and we have seen it, and bear witness, and show unto you that eternal life, which was with the Father, and was manifested unto us;) That which we have seen and heard declare we unto you, that ye also may have fellowship with us: and truly our fellowship is with the Father, and with his Son Jesus Christ. (1 John 1:1-3)*

> *"How can this be?" Nicodemus asked. "You are Israel's teacher," said Jesus, "and do you not understand these things?* **I tell you the truth, we speak of what we know, and we testify to what we have seen,** *but still you people do not accept our testimony. I have*

spoken to you of earthly things and you do not believe; how then will you believe if I speak of heavenly things?" (John 3:9-12 NIV)

Just prior to his ascension, Jesus relayed this message to his disciples:

And he said unto them, **These are the words which I spake unto you,** *while I was yet with you,* **that all things must be fulfilled, which were written in the law of Moses, and in the prophets, and in the psalms, concerning me.** **Then opened he their understanding, that they might understand the scriptures,** *And said unto them, Thus it is written, and thus it behooved Christ to suffer, and to rise from the dead the third day: And that repentance and remission of sins should be preached in his name among all nations, beginning at Jerusalem.* **And ye are witnesses of these things.** *And, behold, I send the promise of my Father upon you: but tarry ye in the city of Jerusalem, until ye be endued with power from on high.*
(Luke 24:44-49)

But ye shall receive power, *after that the Holy Ghost is come upon you:* **and ye shall be witnesses unto me both in Jerusalem,**

and in all Judaea, and in Samaria, and unto the uttermost part of the earth. (Acts 1:8)

This must be our prayer continuously, "Lord, open my heart to understand and see the Scriptures that refer to you." Without the gifts of understanding, faith, charity, wisdom, righteousness and truth, the spirit of prophecy [the testimony of Jesus Christ] is but a history lesson. Our ability to see Jesus throughout the Scriptures is a proof that we have this precious gift. We have an example of this in the book of Acts:

Then the Spirit said unto Philip, Go near, and join thyself to this chariot. And Philip ran thither to him, and heard him read the prophet Esaias, and said, Understandest thou what thou readest? And he said, How can I, except some man should guide me? And he desired Philip that he would come up and sit with him. The place of the scripture which he read was this, *"He was led as a sheep to the slaughter; and like a lamb dumb before his shearer, so opened he not his mouth: In his humiliation his judgment was taken away: and who shall declare his generation? for his life is taken from the earth.*" And the eunuch answered Philip, and said, I pray thee, of whom speaketh the prophet this? of himself, or of some other man? Then Philip opened his mouth, and began at the same scripture, and preached unto him Jesus. (Acts 8:29 – 35)

There are many doctrines concerning the Holy Spirit and his function in the body of Christ and I don't intend to engage in the discussion here. However, I will say this from personal experience: Without being endowed with the power of God from on high, there is no possibility of becoming a true witness for his name's sake.

> *When Jesus came into the coasts of Caesarea Philippi, he asked his disciples, saying, Whom do men say that I the Son of man am? And they said, Some say that thou art John the Baptist: some, Elias; and others, Jeremias, or one of the prophets.*
> *He saith unto them, But whom say ye that I am? And Simon Peter answered and said, Thou art the Christ, the Son of the living God. And Jesus answered and said unto him, Blessed art thou, Simon Barjona: for flesh and blood hath not revealed it unto thee, but my Father which is in heaven.* (Mat 16:13-17)

In Luke 9:18-21 Jesus commanded his disciples not to tell the people that he was the Christ, the Messiah of God. Why; because he did not come to fulfill the role of Messiah. He came to fulfill the role of the Lamb of God. This is why Jesus said that there was no other prophet as great as John the Baptist [excluding himself] because John was able to recognize Jesus and introduce him to the world saying, "Behold the Lamb of God!" All of the writings in the Book of Revelations give honor and glory to the Lamb that was slain for the sin of the world.

Jesus will come in the future and take up the shield and sword as the Lord of Hosts, the King of Glory, the Messiah of Israel, and Ruler over all the earth. This is the testimony of Jesus according to truth, not imaginary beliefs. **God sent the Lamb, not the man**, to be a propitiation for the sin of mankind, for the Jew first, and also the Gentile.

By misrepresenting the purpose of Jesus Christ's epiphany the church has placed a stumbling block before the Jews. Their sages have taught them that the coming Messiah, the Anointed One, will gather an army of trained fighters to drive the enemies of Israel off their land and establish the kingdom of Israel on earth; and so he shall. Jesus did not fulfill that role 2,000 years ago. He was to be treated as any other "man" — accused, judged, and condemned to be crucified by the Romans. However, the Messiah will not suffer a like fate; for he is coming again as the Commander-in-Chief, the Deliverer, and Savior upon whose thigh will be written THE WORD OF GOD. Furthermore, as the Jews readily assert, it is written that one cannot die for the sins of another man.

> *What do you people mean by quoting this proverb about the land of Israel: "'The fathers eat sour grapes, and the children's teeth are set on edge'?" As surely as I live, declares the Sovereign LORD, you will no longer quote this proverb in Israel. For every living soul belongs to me, the father as well as the son--both alike belong to me. The soul who sins is the one who will die.*
> (Ezek 18:2-4 NIV)

> *The soul that sinneth, it shall die. **The son shall not bear the iniquity of the father, neither shall the father bear the iniquity of***

the son: *the righteousness of the righteous shall be upon him, and the wickedness of the wicked shall be upon him.* (Ezek 18:20 NIV)

This is one of the strongest arguments they present to condemn the teaching that Jesus died for the sins of mankind because the Lord spoke through the prophet condemning this doctrine as being alien to the Father's teaching and contrary to the written word. But, those of us who are privy to the Lord's will can see and understand that God permitted the lamb's blood to be shed in place of a man's upon the altar of sacrifice. The very first lamb's sacrifice substituting for the blood of man was recorded in Genesis when the goat was given by the Lord in place of Isaac. This is but an example of seeing the Lord Jesus Christ in the Scriptures according to truth.

Now once we are stripped of all our diverse beliefs in Jesus Christ, most of which are incapable of being validated, what are we left with? Speaking for myself, among many proofs I had to retain in order to bear witness of the Living Savior and the works of the Father in him; I was left with this final statement: "If there is a god who is more perfect, more pure, more holy than the God I have come to know, I cannot fathom his reality. What can be more perfect than perfection itself? What can be more pure than purity itself? And, what can be more holy than holiness itself? If there is an answer to these questions, my intellect cannot bear it. It would be so far above my comprehension to qualify another god as Lord that it would be utterly impossible for me to grasp."

Like all of the gifts and abilities attributed to God, prophecy is a trinity in its essence. The qualities of prophecy include discernment, knowledge of the holy, and the rod of judgment to be executed on the Lord's enemies.

Many believers struggle with this Trinitarian principle; however, everything created by God is triune in consistency. Atoms consist of neutrons, protons, and electrons. If we separate one of the components we no longer have an atom. The human being consists of a body, the spirit that enables it to move, breathe, etc. and blood. The same is true for animals. Vegetation requires a nucleus wherein dwells the energy and mechanism for breathing and reproduction, the exterior membrane, and life maintaining fluid such as cytoplasm. If we remove one of these components it will result in the death of the plant, animal, or human. Space consists of length, depth and width. Time involves the present, past, and future. Everything created by God in its natural order was created in his image and likeness, and nature verifies his Trinitarian form.

This is one of the proofs by the way, to determine if a messenger is speaking the word of God. He will declare the Father working through the Son by the power and might of the Holy Spirit: not Jesus only, Jehovah only, or the Holy Spirit only. In the first chapter of Ephesians, Paul gives us a teaching magnifying this truth.

I agree with Paul that prophecy is the greater gift, but I must add that it is the most difficult to acquire. Prophecy, Wisdom, Faith, Charity, and every good gift comes from God: and while it is said that God gives them to the church to profit thereby, the word would probably be best taught as "God vests [trusts] the church with his gifts for the success of his work and the edification and multiplication of his body, the Israel of God."

In Christ we find everything that was made, and in him dwells all the fullness of the Godhead in bodily form. There are many so-called inconsistencies in the Scripture that would be easily translated if the person had the gift of prophecy and could see the person of Christ being glorified throughout the Living Word.

To recap, Truth is a living persona, and prophecy validates this persona as the image of the invisible God, witnessed by holy men of God endowed with the wisdom, vision, and faith that comes through Jesus Christ to declare him. This truth can only be discovered in Christ, in his doctrines, in his faith, which we call Christianity. There is no other faith that teaches these truths.

Everyone who wishes to become a true witness for Christ must be willing to surrender all of his intellect, past instructions, and beliefs to the Lord without hesitation so that he can teach us the truths necessary to become a true witness of him. Why; because, as I said earlier, the trials are intense; and there is absolutely no room for unfounded beliefs, opinions, ideas, commentaries, and suppositions. For our own protection we must make sure that we are dwelling in the fullness of His light where we will be educated in His wisdom and truth. It isn't my intent to dissuade anyone from seeking the Lord and his truths; however, I feel that it's important to urge everyone to be fully prepared for the difficulties you will experience. As St. Paul would say, be strengthened with his might in the inner man. To identify and proclaim the presence of the invisible Jesus Christ to a world who believes they can see and hear to the glory of Almighty God is truly the greatest of all gifts.

THE ISRAEL OF GOD

Generally, when the name Israel is mentioned our thoughts tend to focus on the land bearing this name, and the Jewish people whose fathers were named the children of Israel in the Scriptures. But, as you should expect by now, this is not the whole truth regarding Israel. God revealed the mystery of the Israel of God to Moses.

> "And thou shalt say unto Pharaoh, Thus saith the LORD, **Israel is my son, even my firstborn:** And I say unto thee, Let my son go, that he may serve me: and if thou refuse to let him go, behold, I will slay thy son, even thy firstborn." (Ex. 4:22,23)

There were more than six hundred thousand men besides women and children, but the Lord consolidated the multitude into one body, his son, Jesus Christ, the Israel of God. God had given Jacob the name Israel, [Prince of God], more than six hundred years earlier, but this was the first time God had called Abraham's seed his own son.

But God forbid that I should glory, save in the cross of our Lord Jesus Christ, by whom the world is crucified unto me, and I unto the world. For in Christ Jesus neither circumcision availeth anything, nor uncircumcision, but a new creature. And as many as walk according to this rule, peace be on them, and mercy, and **upon the Israel of God.**
(Gal 6:14-16)

The Israel of God is comprised of all believers whose God is the God of Abraham, the one true God.

As for me, this is my covenant with you: **You will be the father of many nations.** *No longer will you be called Abram; your name will be Abraham,* **for I have made you a father of many nations.** *I will make you very fruitful;* **I will make nations of you, and kings will come from you. I will establish my covenant as an everlasting covenant between me and you and your descendants after you for the generations to come, to be your God and the God of your descendants after you. The whole land of Canaan, where you are now an alien, I will give as an everlasting possession to you and your descendants after you; and I will be their God.** *(Gen.17.4 -8 NIV)*

"I *must be* [or will be] their God." This was the contingency God inserted into the Covenant and restated it three times so there could be no misunderstanding. The inheritance granted to Abraham and his seed only applied to those who made Abraham's God, their God. Why do you suppose the Lord dispossessed the Israelites from their land when they worshipped other gods? It makes no difference if one is a genealogical descendant of Abraham or a Gentile convert; the people of faith are counted as one in the Israel of God.

> *Therefore, remember that formerly you who are Gentiles by birth and called "uncircumcised" by those who call themselves "the circumcision" (that done in the body by the hands of men)--**remember that at that time you were separate from Christ, excluded from citizenship in Israel and foreigners to the covenants of the promise, without hope and without God in the world. But now in Christ Jesus you who once were far away have been brought near through the blood of Christ. For <u>he himself is our peace, who has made the two one and has destroyed the barrier, the dividing wall of hostility,</u>** by abolishing in his flesh the law with its commandments and*

regulations. ***His purpose was to create in himself one new man out of the two,*** *thus making peace, and* ***in this one body to reconcile both of them to God through the cross,*** *by which he put to death their* ***hostility.*** *He came and preached peace to you who were far away and peace to those who were near.* ***For through him we both*** **[Jew and Gentile]** ***have access to the Father by one Spirit.*** *Consequently,* ***you are no longer foreigners and aliens, but fellow citizens with God's people and members of God's household,*** *built on the foundation of the apostles and prophets, with Christ Jesus himself as the chief cornerstone. In him the whole building is joined together and rises to become a holy temple in the Lord. And in him you too are being built together to become a dwelling in which God lives by his Spirit.*
(Eph 2:11-22 NIV)

Now, if Jesus Christ has made peace between the Israelite and Gentile nations, what spirit entices us to foster hostility, jealousy, and prejudice between the peoples? What do we make ourselves that we should oppose the will of God and decide to rebuild the wall of enmity and resurrect that which was made dead in Christ Jesus by his death on the cross?

A child of God is not one only on the outward appearance; nor is he one who professes his faith in Christ then demonstrates his true faith by engaging in the sins of the flesh. No, a child of God is one inwardly, whose faith is evidenced by the righteous works of God accomplished through faith in Christ in the inner man, in the heart; not by works born out of necessity, obligation, and religious mandates.

All of the promises are contingent, not upon the Holy Seed being religious, or belonging to a particular church or temple, but on the Seed of Abraham being filled with faith, devotion, and commitment to the God of Abraham—that he will be our God. So then, it is not by an outward show of righteousness that we are fellow heirs with the household of faith, but an inner faith in the Father and in his Son, Jesus Christ and the outward "glow" of righteousness because he is in us and we are in him..

> But God found fault with the people and said; "The time is coming, declares the Lord, when I will make a new covenant with the house of Israel and with the house of Judah. It will not be like the covenant I made with

*their forefathers when I took them by the hand to lead them out of Egypt, because they did not remain faithful to my covenant, and I turned away from them, declares the Lord. **This is the covenant I will make with the house of Israel after that time, declares the Lord. I will put my laws in their minds and write them on their hearts. I will be their God, and they will be my people.***
(Heb 8:8-10 NIV)

***Know ye therefore that they which are of faith, the same are the children of Abraham.** And the scripture, foreseeing that **God would justify the heathen through faith, preached before the gospel unto Abraham,** saying, In thee shall all nations be blessed. So then they which be of faith are blessed with faithful Abraham. (Gal 3:7-9)*

*Now to Abraham and his seed were the promises made. He saith not, And to seeds, as of many; but as of one, **And to thy seed, which is Christ.** (Gal 3:16)*

Now if the Seed is Christ, and the Seed of Promise came by Abraham, then the Israel of God is not one who clings to a religion, whether he is Jew or Gentile; but those of us who have been called to the heavenly kingdom, made to be partakers of the covenants of promise and given an inheritance by virtue of the adoption of sons which was confirmed in Christ – the Israel and Son of the Most High God— because of our faith, commitment to holiness, and loyalty to the Father who made our adoption possible.

> *"For I know the plans I have for you,"* *declares the LORD, "plans to prosper you and not to harm you, plans to give you hope and a future. Then you will call upon me and come and pray to me, and I will listen to you. You will seek me and find me when you seek me with all your heart." (Jer. 29:11-13 NIV)*

It has always been God's will to have One Seed, One Tree of Life, One Communion, rooted and grounded in the love of God; One Family, with many strong branches bearing the fruits of righteousness, faith, truth and love—ultimately One Kingdom, ruled by One King—the Lord Almighty. To accomplish this, he set the following plan in motion.

He planted his family in the land of Canaan and confirmed Abraham as its founding father. From Canaan, God said he would increase Abraham's seed to exceedingly vast numbers, compelling them to expand their borders from generation to generation, until the entire earth was occupied with Abraham's seed. This was the plan God was referring to when he told Abraham to count the stars if he was able, because his seed would be that numerous. When the plan of worldwide expansion would be accomplished, God's promise that Abraham would become the father of many nations, and that all the earth would be blessed in him, would be fulfilled; and, of course, our God would reign as Lord and King over all the earth. This was, is, and forever will be—God's plan!

The liberals and unbelievers make a mockery of this plan, calling it Utopian and impossible to fulfill. What they fail to realize is the God of wisdom is incapable of devising a plan that is impossible to accomplish. Is God to blame for this plan not succeeding through the centuries? Or, do we point to the Adversary for setting up his pawns in positions of authority, having them distort the words and the will of God, and commanding his "leaders" to guide the people in the doctrines of prosperity, propaganda, and self-gratification? Was it God or his adversary that perpetuated jealousy, anger and hate for one another until the nations engaged in all-out war?

It was always the adversary's intent to conquer Jerusalem, the throne of the Lord, for himself, and cause all the earth to worship the beast instead of the Creator. His plan has been in motion for many, many centuries, but thanks be to God he hasn't succeeded. But the time is coming, and is upon us, when the Holy Seed will be separated from the wicked, and then the ungodly one will be revealed, whose coming is from the pit of darkness. He will have his final chance to bind and hold captive those who refuse to believe in the truth, and find consolation in believing a lie.

Compare the similarity between these two statements: 1) God's plan, [what many are taught and compelled to believe], provides for the establishment of one true religion and culture. 2) God's plan, [his truth], provides for the perpetuation of one family joined in heart and spirit; one nation of many peoples, having one identity, joint heirs, and co-citizens of God's Kingdom, sharing the inheritance of their father, and benefitting from the presence and blessings of God—the rewards of their love, respect, and devotion to him, and the free exercise of charity one towards the other.

As we look back at the two statements of "faith", above, which one illuminates the nature of a God of love, grace, mercy, and everlasting righteousness? In addition, which one would lead people to believe that God is prejudiced, biased, and discriminatory? This is the difference between religious doctrines everyone must "accept by faith" because they may find a sentence in Scripture that seemingly gives some "factual credibility" to their argument.

God's truth expresses the faithfulness of His grace and mercy in his acceptance of us; exposes his willingness to bless us and allows us to share in the fulfillment of his love; enabling us to experience his joys and delights, his happiness, freedoms, and security. Which of the two scenarios would make us ask this question of the Lord? "Why did you bring me

into this world, and allow me to be born to a ----------
who is not of the one true religion and culture?" You
may say, "Who can question God?" But, let's be real!
I have a hard time picturing myself, or anyone else
for that matter, standing before the Judge of all the
earth, being denied entrance into his kingdom, simply
because I did not meet the specifications of culture,
or religion; and not question his "righteous
judgment." In fact, let's take a page from the
teachings of Jesus who gave us an interesting lesson
concerning this issue. He said,

> *All the nations will be gathered before him,*
> *and he will separate the people one from*
> *another as a shepherd separates the sheep*
> *from the goats. He will put the sheep on his*
> *right and the goats on his left. Then the King*
> *will say to those on his right, 'Come, you who*
> *are blessed by my Father; take your*
> *inheritance, the kingdom prepared for you*
> *since the creation of the world. For I was*
> *hungry and you gave me something to eat, I*
> *was thirsty and you gave me something to*
> *drink, I was a stranger and you invited me in,*
> *I needed clothes and you clothed me, I was*
> *sick and you looked after me, I was in prison*

and you came to visit me.' **_Then the righteous will answer him, 'Lord, when did we see you hungry and feed you, or thirsty and give you something to drink? When did we see you a stranger and invite you in, or needing clothes and clothe you? When did we see you sick or in prison and go to visit you?'_** *The King will reply, 'I tell you the truth, whatever you did for one of the least of these brothers of mine, you did for me.' Then he will say to those on his left, 'Depart from me, you who are cursed, into the eternal fire prepared for the devil and his angels. For I was hungry and you gave me nothing to eat, I was thirsty and you gave me nothing to drink, I was a stranger and you did not invite me in, I needed clothes and you did not clothe me, I was sick and in prison and you did not look after me.'* **_They also will answer, 'Lord, when did we see you hungry or thirsty or a stranger or needing clothes or sick or in prison, and did not help you?'_** *He will reply, 'I tell you the truth, whatever you did not do for one of the least of these, you did not do for me.' Then they will go away to eternal punishment, but the righteous to eternal life.* (Matt.25:32-46 NIV)

[Take note: Jesus said that not only the accursed, but also the righteous will question his decision on that day!] Now, I can't imagine questioning the Lord's decision when he is welcoming me into his kingdom. I can only surmise that it must be one of those imperfections imbedded in our human nature. So, imagine the outcry if he said we didn't belong to the proper religious group or culture!

As we saw in Jesus' teaching there was no mention of culture or religion. All he spoke about was the charitable work of Godly righteousness—putting the needs, cares, and concerns of the needy before one self.

Take a good look at the country we, the Israel of God, live in and ask the following questions: Are the poor being schooled in a vocation that will permit them to dig themselves out of the pit of despair and gloom? Is the economy stable? Is the nation in serious debt? Are the youth being disciplined and raised with respect, honor, and decency toward people, property, and leadership? Is the society permissive? Are a great number of children being born out of wedlock; or perhaps being aborted? Is the nation safe and secure from terroristic threats from foreign and domestic gangs?

Now, take a look at the government officials. Are they promoting solutions to these problems? Are they encouraging faith in Christ, or are they prohibiting free worship? Are more people being killed on a daily basis in the country than are being reconciled to their heavenly father? Are preachers, rabbis and imams spreading hate and distrust among the people? Now you have an excellent picture of your nation and its leadership. The same situations are prevalent in every country, so where do you go to escape?

Christians have the Spirit with them to bring down preachers and leaders who oppose the principles of Christ and set up those whose hearts have been circumcised to understand truth, care for the poor, uphold the name and principled teachings of Jesus Christ, and set the nation back on a solid foundation. This is the work of God in the Christians who take responsibility for the upbringing of their children, and the stability and security of their nation; Christians who have the courage and faith to suffer persecution for the glory of God.

As the Holy Seed gathers in Jesus' name and yields to his Holy Spirit, we will begin to witness his mighty hand at work, become viable participants in his plan, and witnesses to its fulfillment. Those of us endowed with a deep inner faith, determination, and conviction in the Almighty God of Abraham must lead the way. The strength of our convictions are found in our works of charity, love, and forgiveness—virtues that spring to life from an inner faith, an upright heart, even the same faith Abraham practiced and found favor with God.

These were some of the teachings of the early church fathers and were among the doctrines believed by the Christians of that day. As you probably have seen, there is at best a slight difference between them and the typical Christian teachings of today.

What does God want from us? He wants us to recognize the fact that as a Christian we are merely a visitor on earth; that our home is in heaven: that we are not bound by Democrat or Republican politics; rather, we are bound to uphold the covenants and commandments of our Lord and Savior, Jesus Christ.

On a more personal note the question is — Am I willing to set aside my personal and political beliefs and rely on the edicts of Scripture as a child of God and citizen of Heaven; casting my vote only for those whose politics are based on the tenets of Scripture? Or, am I willing to just go along to get along? As you have seen, we have several decisions to make that will ultimately determine the extent of our relationship with God.

My hope is that you have witnessed New Testament teachings in a new light and realize that every doctrine was given to the apostles for the benefit of the Church and His ministry so that we may all come in unity of the faith. And it is also my hope that you have decided to go all the way for Christ— even as he went all the way for you. God bless.

www.ingramcontent.com/pod-product-compliance
Lightning Source LLC
Chambersburg PA
CBHW061742020426

42331CB00006B/1329